EXPLORING VALUES

RELEASING THE POWER OF ATTITUDES

by JUDY SUITER

Competitive Edge, Inc.
P.O. Box 2418 • Peachtree City, GA 30269
www.competitiveedgeinc.com

TABLE OF CONTENTS

DEDICATION

To my sons, Brett and Drew, who are the essence of my being.

ACKNOWLEDGMENTS

There are so many people who have enriched my life over the years, and I sincerely value their friendship, professional guidance, and constant encouragement. These caring individuals have enabled me to spend the last twenty years in the most rewarding life's work that I could ever have imagined, and I would like to acknowledge them for their contributions to my endeavors.

I express my heartfelt thanks to Pat and Bob Bender, Judy Beazley, Jim Cecil, Patricia and Phil Colston, Ivory Dorsey, Dr. Mike and Anna Fields, Dean Gentry, Jackie Goldammer, E.A. Gresham, George Haberkern, Beverly and Ed Hay, Barbara and Jim Hughes, Marie Kane, Alberta Lloyd, Dudley Lynch, Lee and Hal Murray, George Myers, Veronica Ross, Earl Suttle, Vern Thomas, Eileen Tooley, Bob Tumperi and Margaret Vail. They have gone above and beyond the ties of friendship and, in their own individual ways, have kept me focused in reality.

I would also like to acknowledge my greatest pro-

---

moters and supporters—my clients: Tom Baily, Larry Clark, Linda Coonrad, and Luis Rodriquez of Medtronic, Inc; Julie Bellamy with ACSYS Technologies; Rob Brown of Thorn Smith Laboratories; Bridgette Crandall of Quaker Oats; Bob Crutchfield and Karen Kilgo of Christian City; Claire Dugger of Mississippi Power Company; Bill Handler of Handler & Associates; LaVerne Johnson of the International Institute of Learning, Inc.; Stephen Perkins with Darden Restaurants; Betty Lou Pigg and Katherine Tankson with the Mississippi Department of Education; John Taylor and Jim Walter from Tyco Healthcare/Mallinckrodt, Inc; Toby Tolbert of Nisshinbo Automotive Manufacturing; Randy Wade of Techspray, Inc.; Linda Wind with Possible Woman; and D. R. Wynkoop with the U.S. Department of Defense. I would be remiss if I didn't also acknowledge the TTI staff and the assistance they have provided to me and my clients over the last fourteen years. All of these special people have continued to believe in the power of my work over many years.

This book would not have been possible without the expertise and patience of Darbie Bufford, my assistant. She painstakingly translated all my handwritten scribbles into a coherent form. When I overextend my strengths, Darbie has learned to tell it like it is and very quickly brings me back to reality. I can always count on Janet Boyce for her editing, proofreading and research assistance. Dr. David

Warburton was the catalyst behind this book, as he convinced me that I did have something truly worthwhile to say. Bill Bonnstetter provided me with the technological tools to assess values and attitudes. Dr. Michael O'Connor taught me the foundations for understanding value systems. To this very unique group of people, I am profoundly grateful.

I also want to acknowledge Catherine Carlisi, who was instrumental in motivating me to write the first edition of this book and helped me with its writing, editing, and proofreading. Catherine is a Certified Behavior Analyst and consultant who worked conscientiously to bring my values and attitudes seminar to print.

Finally, I want to thank my mother, the late Lois Bohlke, for her total and unconditional love and encouragement, and my sister, Linda Miller, who provided me with my "first experiences" in behavior and values differences. Linda continues to enrich my training programs by giving me numerous real life examples of these concepts.

INTRODUCTION

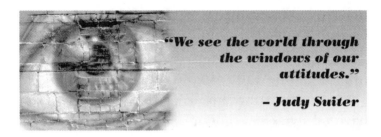

"We see the world through the windows of our attitudes."

– Judy Suiter

WHY LEARN ABOUT VALUES AND ATTITUDES?

Most of us do not go through life alone—on a daily basis, we interact with others on the job and in our public and personal lives. Positive relationships with bosses, co-workers, and business contacts such as clients, customers, and suppliers can help create favorable work experiences and contribute to career success. Healthy relationships with spouses or significant others, children, in-laws, and friends create joy and balance in our lives and can provide a safe haven from the stresses of modern life. Without insight or training, we generally tend to enjoy conversations and activities with people who have attitudes and values similar to our own and may experience conflicts with people of differing attitudes.

We relate most effectively and expend the least

energy trying to cope with or resolve conflict situations when we understand the motivating factors that drive human behavior. In other words, when we truly understand why people do the things they do, we are likely to bring a higher level of resourcefulness and flexibility to our interactions—and get better results. For example, people with certain behavioral styles are sometimes considered to be poor listeners. But when you attune your message to their values and passions, they will become "all ears." The study of behavior and values is not an exact science, but there is a methodology that contributes to the art of "people reading" and provides a foundation for improved interpersonal skills and acceptance of differences.

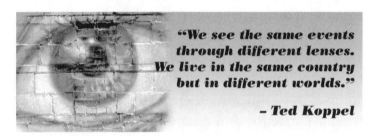

"We see the same events through different lenses. We live in the same country but in different worlds."

– Ted Koppel

The behavioral aspect of people-reading is discussed in the first booklet of this series, entitled *Energizing People: Unleashing the Power of DISC.* In this book, *Exploring Values: Releasing the Power of Attitudes,* we investigate the hidden motivators that drive behavior. A skilled observer can accurately assess others' behavioral styles, or how they do things,

---

through their body language, words, voice tone and pace. Why humans do things is values-driven and is invisible. Values and attitudes are usually revealed only through discussion, as people disclose their rationale for the choices and decisions they make.

Learning how to elicit and understand others' attitudes and values is a skill with many practical applications, not the least of which is creating mutually beneficial relationships. Understanding our own invisible drivers can literally change our lives by giving us more conscious choices over the decisions we make. You can think of *Exploring Values: Releasing the Power of Attitudes* as a travel guide that provides you with a glimpse into the customs and worldviews of people from different lands, though the geography is within our heads and hearts.

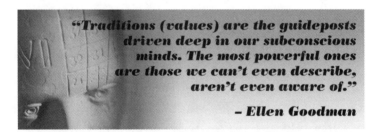

"Traditions (values) are the guideposts driven deep in our subconscious minds. The most powerful ones are those we can't even describe, aren't even aware of."

– Ellen Goodman

HOW CAN UNDERSTANDING OUR OWN MOTIVATORS GIVE US MORE CHOICE OVER DECISIONS?

At any given time, either needs or values will be the primary force behind a person's actions. When

---

a conflict occurs between needs and values, research shows that needs-fulfillment usually dominates over values, except when a person is sufficiently self-aware to make a choice to act from the perspective of their values systems. When you understand your own values perspective, you are able to assess both the short-term and long-term consequences of your decisions, not only in relation to personal needs, but also to your sense of identity and broader considerations of ethics, integrity, or life purpose.

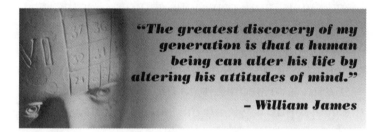

"The greatest discovery of my generation is that a human being can alter his life by altering his attitudes of mind."

– William James

HOW ARE ATTITUDES, BELIEFS AND VALUES DEVELOPED?

Researchers say that attitudes, beliefs and values develop through stages, from childhood to adulthood, and are related to stimuli such as conflict, stress, or even pain. They can also develop through experiences of pleasure, satisfaction, and joy. We instantly, and often unconsciously, create beliefs in response to things we see, hear, and experience throughout our lives. These beliefs tend to cluster together and increase in intensity and feelings, evolving into a hierarchy of attitudes—our unique positive and negative viewpoints. These attitudes eventually create the purpose and direction for our lives.

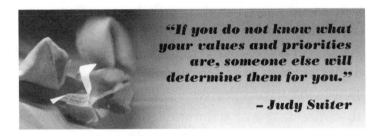

"If you do not know what your values and priorities are, someone else will determine them for you."

– Judy Suiter

WHAT ARE THE DIFFERENT LEVELS OF MOTIVATION?

Abraham Maslow, in his landmark works, *Toward a Psychology of Being* (1962) and *Motivation and Personality* (1970), identified five basic levels of needs through which all people have the capability of progressing as part of their personal evolution—physical survival, safety, social, esteem and self-actualization. His Hierarchy of Needs is depicted in the pyramid below.

MASLOW'S HIERARCHY OF NEEDS

5 Self-Actualization
4 Esteem
3 Social
2 Safety
1 Survival

In Maslow's first stage of needs, basic survival is the overriding concern, and efforts are focused on obtaining food, water, shelter, and clothing.

Once survival needs are met, people become focused on safety, both physical and psychological, which is the second level of needs. Because these first stages are so linked to the survival of the individual, those who put the interests of others above their own survival needs, as is sometimes seen during times of war or natural disaster, are celebrated as heroes. In order to make such choices, heroes usually must be operating from one of the higher orders of needs in the top half of Maslow's hierarchy. As long as individuals are working to satisfy their self-oriented, primary needs, they are not likely to operate or make choices that are based in an others-oriented values perspective.

The third stage of Maslow's hierarchy is what he called social or "belongingness," the sense of being part of a group or family. For example, our need for belonging can be satisfied in the workplace through an organization's team-oriented culture or, in our personal lives, through identification with a political party, ethnic group, church or community.

Once individuals reach the fourth stage of development, which Maslow identified as the need for self-esteem, they are more likely to be influenced by a transcendent order of needs. Once they are given the relevant information, people have the capacity to expand their perspectives and make choices that better serve long-term survival and the more intrinsic human needs. At this point, the focus begins to shift from gratification of personal needs to redefining self through interaction with and service to others. This stage incorporates the concept of self-worth with the concept of self-respect—not only do I feel good about the fact that I can meet the needs of others and myself, but I respect the way I fulfill those needs.

According to Maslow, the fifth and highest level of aspiration is the state of self-actualization, the full expression of human potential. Those who operate from this wider frame of reference may be involved in global issues with far-reaching consequences, or they may have dedicated their lives to an inner journey that transcends the day-to-day concerns of "average" people. They are often generous of spirit, unusually resilient, and live life with a sense of mission. In his personal research, Maslow determined that only three percent of the population ever reaches the stage of self-actualization.

Based on life circumstances, it is also possible to revert to a more basic need level, such as survival or safety. The foundation of the pyramid must be stabilized. Then, once the need is again satisfied, we may operate from a more values-driven perspective. An example of how we can go up and down the "needs ladder" would be when people who lose their jobs begin to suffer from a loss of self-esteem and, for a time, may even become anxious about their ability to pay the mortgage or meet other basic survival needs. Once gainful employment is restored, these fears dissipate, self-esteem is restored, and the individual once more turns attention to operating from their values/beliefs.

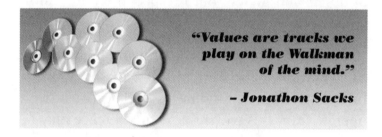

"Values are tracks we play on the Walkman of the mind."

– Jonathon Sacks

HOW DO THE VALUES CLUSTERS RELATE TO BEHAVIORAL STYLES?

Metaphorically, behavioral styles are the doorway to understanding others, and values clusters are the arenas in which communication occurs. Attitudes and values drive behaviors; actions are carried out in response to basic human needs.

For example, individuals may declare that they want to be successful in a chosen field. *Why* they want to be successful is driven by their values or attitudes. *How* they go about accomplishing their intention is a function of their behavioral style, and the ways by which they achieve their success will reflect the characteristics of that style.

How people strive to satisfy their needs is determined by their different behavioral styles: high "D" styles tend to be directive and results-oriented; the high "I" behavioral tendency is to seek out and interact with people; high "S" styles have a need for steadiness and security; and high "C" behavioral styles tend to set and comply with their own high standards. (For more information on behavioral styles, refer to *Energizing People—Unleashing the Power of DISC.*)

The passions that drive people to move up Maslow's hierarchy were researched and defined as *Theoretical, Utilitarian, Aesthetic, Social, Individualistic*, and *Traditional* by Eduard Spranger, who presented his findings in the book, *Types of Men*, published in 1928.

Generally, the most compelling two passions become our primary motivators and tend to influence the other four. These passions, also known as *values clusters*, are the subject of this booklet. Values clusters are dynamic and can become relatively more or less important, based upon significant changes in an individual's life circumstances.

The Personal Interests, Attitudes and Values

(PIAV) assessment tool provides a snapshot of your current values-based drivers. Your primary values are the ones through which you filter the information you utilize in decision-making.

In coming chapters, we will look at the characteristics of each of the six values clusters, as well as some of the practical applications and the potential stresses that relate to each. Because stories help people learn, I have illustrated these sections with examples. Please note that I have used the terms "attitudes," "drives," and "values clusters" interchangeably for purposes of this text.

"Strong lives are motivated by dynamic purposes."

– Kenneth Hildebrand

THEORETICAL
VALUES CLUSTER

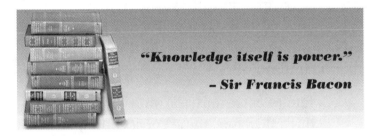

"Knowledge itself is power."

– Sir Francis Bacon

People with a high *Theoretical* values cluster love ideas and exploring new interests. They rarely walk by a bookstore without stopping in, usually come out loaded down with books, and may have trouble putting a good book down. People with a high *Theoretical* values cluster thirst for information on a wide range of subjects for the sake of the knowledge itself. If they turn on the television, they prefer to watch The Discovery Channel or The History Channel, or they may choose to watch programs like *Jeopardy* or *National Geographic Explorer*. This thirst for knowledge also provides a high *Theoretical* with a greater sense of objectivity, sharper critical thinking skills, and the ability to debate on a more rational level.

Many of the great thinkers and philosophers of the world have been motivated by a high *Theoretical* values cluster. For example, the Twilight Club is an organization founded more than a hundred years ago by a group of visionary thinkers whose membership has included such luminaries as Andrew Carnegie, Ralph Waldo Emerson, Walt Whitman, and Mark Twain. Their high *Theoretical* underpinnings are revealed in this excerpt from their manifesto:

> "Commitment to universal truth is the hallmark of ethics; therefore, the act of assuming the responsibility of thinking in pursuit of universal truth is the foundational ethical virtue."

But the Twilight Club also has a strong *Social* aspect, as demonstrated in this additional quote from their charter, in which *Theoretical* considerations are augmented by responsibility toward others:

> "Human beings are at their best not when they are engaged in abstract reflection, or when they are engaged in individual transformation for its own sake, but when they are engaged in action to transform the corners of the world in which they live."

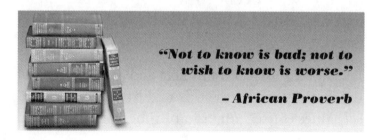

"Not to know is bad; not to wish to know is worse."

– African Proverb

A good example of an individual with strong *Theoretical* and *Social* values clusters is Oprah Winfrey. Oprah's high *Theoretical* values perspective is reflected in her love of books and the very popular magazine she has launched. (Oprah's Book Club is the literary seal of approval for millions of her fans and has been credited with putting many books on the bestseller list.) Her companion values cluster, high *Social*, has shaped the types of books she recommends and the articles she accepts for publication in her magazine. Listening to her comments during interviews and observing where she puts her considerable energy, we can surmise that Oprah is expressing strong *Theoretical* values through her high *Social* values to create a better world for others through education.

Lifelong learning is the only assurance of lifelong employment.

André Larochelle

Consider Theodore Roosevelt, the 26th President of the United States, known not only for his great energy, but for his passion for knowledge in far-ranging subjects. He is acknowledged as an essayist, a physical culturalist, a naval historian, a civil service reformer, a patron of the arts, and an outstanding military expert. Roosevelt is known to have written over 150,000 letters to express his thoughts and ideas during his lifetime. Reading was a daily habit, and he sometimes read as many as three books in one day. His interest in big game hunting coincided with his love of the American environment. During his presidency, he created five new national parks, which suggests that he probably had a high *Aesthetic* values cluster as well.

In contrast, individuals with a low *Theoretical* drive will learn things only if they see an immediate practical application of the knowledge, or if there is a specific area of study that intrigues them, such as gardening or American history. Some may even achieve the status of expert in their area of passion, but their *Theoretical* drive is "situational," rather than high.

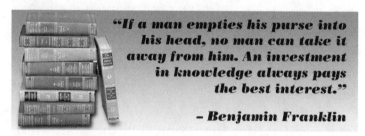

"If a man empties his purse into his head, no man can take it away from him. An investment in knowledge always pays the best interest."

– Benjamin Franklin

Occasionally, thirst for knowledge can create conflicts with other life considerations. I once received a distressed telephone call from a colleague who knew that I, too, operated from a high *Theo-*

retical values cluster. He told me, "You are the only one I know in the world who will understand the terrible dilemma I'm facing," He had been running his own consulting company while concurrently working toward a Ph.D. For many of us, juggling two such demanding endeavors would be a challenge, but his situation was even more perplexing. His Ph.D. course work was so engrossing that he felt driven to devote more and more time to his studies and was neglecting his work. Eventually, he found himself resisting efforts to schedule the very consulting work that was funding his scholastic endeavors. This is an example of a strong values preference taken to extremes, which can cause intrapersonal conflicts.

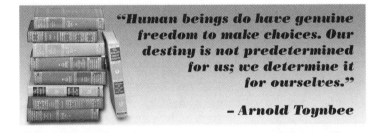

"Human beings do have genuine freedom to make choices. Our destiny is not predetermined for us; we determine it for ourselves."

– Arnold Toynbee

Because they want to stay current on a variety of topics, individuals with a high *Theoretical* attitude usually subscribe to numerous magazines. However, with the busy lives most of them lead, they may not find time to read all of them. If they also have a high *Utilitarian* attitude, they will experience guilt over wasting financial resources. As information seems to double at the speed of light, individuals who do not understand their high *Theoretical* passion will most likely experience increased levels of stress as a result of trying to keep abreast of the information and with the technology needed to access it.

UTILITARIAN
VALUES CLUSTER

"Money swore an oath that nobody who didn't love it should ever have it."

– Irish Proverb

The *Utilitarian* values cluster is best characterized by the desire for wealth and an expectation of return on all investments of time, energy or money. Our country's history is replete with examples of self-made men who used their wits and wills to amass huge personal fortunes. The names of Astor, Vanderbilt, Carnegie, Hearst, and Rockefeller are some of those who became legendary by ruthlessly leading their businesses and destroying their competition in the race for riches. (Later in life, many of them also became great philanthropists, a phenomenon we will address later).

The first U.S. billionaire was John D. Rockefeller, whose Standard Oil Company was eventually broken up into Mobil, Exxon, Chevron, and other oil giants that still dominate the industry. J.P. Morgan, the most famous banker in the world, used his personal fortune to save the developing United States economy from severe depression on more than one occasion. Morgan also organized the formation of U.S. Steel, the world's first billion-dollar corporation.

Bill Gates, billionaire founder and largest shareholder of Microsoft, is the epitome of an individual operating out of the *Utilitarian* values cluster, and he runs his company on the same principles. People employed by Microsoft know they will consistently work extremely long hours but that their efforts will pay off in the opportunity to become millionaires themselves, as many Microsoft employees have already done.

> *"America's abundance was not created by public sacrifices to the public good but by the productive genius of free men who pursued their own personal interests and the making of their own private fortunes."*
>
> **– Ayn Rand**

For such high achievers, failure to meet personal goals can be devastating, even when they appear to be excelling in the eyes of the world. My colleague, Catherine Carlisi, had an acquaintance who told her about the only time she ever saw her former husband cry. He was a successful commercial airline pilot, who, on his birthday, had to face that he had not achieved his goal of amassing a million dollars by age thirty. His wife had very different values clusters and had been struggling to cope with two babies without the most basic of conveniences because of his extreme frugality. Feeling resentment, she could neither understand nor sympathize with his disappointment.

In some cases the conservation of resources, rather than the acquisition of wealth, is emphasized in the *Utilitarian* values cluster. Are you the type of person who usually walks out of a restaurant with a doggy bag because you wouldn't dream of wasting the good food for which you paid? Do you have to bite your tongue not to ask for your companion's untouched goodies as well? This everyday indicator is a good clue about whether or not you are motivated by a high *Utilitarian* drive.

Once, a consultant friend, his wife and I went out for dinner. The consultant couldn't finish his meal, but didn't want to look cheap in front of me, so he resisted the temptation to ask for a doggy bag. I, who knew my friend had a high *Utilitarian* drive, suggested that he take home the leftovers. He was thrilled to be able to act on his preference—and quickly turned to his wife, who hadn't finished her meal, either, and asked if she would like to take her leftovers home, too. "No," she replied quickly, "I've had all I want." Laughing, I said to my friend, "You didn't have to ask that. You know your wife has a low *Utilitarian* values cluster, so she would never ask for a doggy bag!" The woman agreed, "You're absolutely right," and chuckled over my insight.

The humorous end of the story results not from different values, but from the associated behavioral styles of each. In the parking lot, the high *Utilitarian*, High "D" (behavioral style) consultant remembered that he hadn't picked up his doggy bag after all. He turned to his wife and asked if she had retrieved it. "Of course, dear," she replied, "I've been picking them up for you for years."

"Money is better than poverty, if only for financial reasons."

– Woody Allen

The conservation aspect of the high *Utilitarian* values cluster sometimes results in ironic, or even humorous, situations. Warren Buffet, despite his $36.5 billion dollars of stock in Berkshire Hathaway, Inc., reportedly still drives an older Lincoln Town Car and lives in the house he bought more than three decades ago. J. Paul Getty, who made more than a billion dollars in the oil business and acquired a very large and valuable art collection, became one of the world's richest men. However, during his lifetime, he was known as an eccentric miser, and one story reveals that he even installed a pay telephone for guests' use at his English mansion!

A more striking example of this conservation aspect of the high *Utilitarian* values cluster is revealed in the behavior of Albert Einstein, who purchased several suits of the same design and color so he would not waste time trying to match things. Others who have a high *Utilitarian* values cluster have a desire to gain wealth rather than conserve it, such as Donald Trump, who is known for speculative real estate purchases that earned him millions when they appreciated.

"If you would be wealthy, think of saving as well as getting."

– Ben Franklin

Coupling this conserving aspect of the *Utilitarian* with a high *Aesthetic* values cluster can result in a strong desire to conserve natural resources in order to preserve the environment. A good example of a company organized around these principles is Earthship Biotecture, which builds entirely self-sustaining homes using recycled materials such as automobile tires filled with com- pacted earth. These homes also have unique power and water treatment systems and feature passive solar heating and cooling.

On the other hand, a low *Utilitarian* drive is ex- emplified in this example of the architect of the World Wide Web—which has changed the world's economy and upon which millions of dollars have been made. Do you know this individual's name? Probably not, because Tim Berners-Lee, the self-ef- facing Englishman who devised a way to quickly and efficiently move documents over the Internet, shuns the limelight. He has turned down many of- fers that would have enabled him to get rich as a result of his invention. When interviewed, Berners- Lee asserts his belief that success and happiness are not measured by financial gain. He works to keep the Internet open and free; clearly, Berners-Lee has a low *Utilitarian* attitude.

AESTHETIC
VALUES CLUSTER

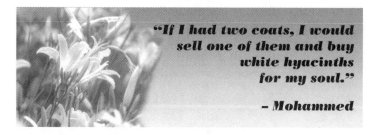

"If I had two coats, I would sell one of them and buy white hyacinths for my soul."

– Mohammed

Attention to form, as well as function, is a trademark of those with a strong *Aesthetic* values cluster. Steven Jobs, co-founder of Apple Computer, is known in the industry as an "aesthetic genius" and demonstrates this by developing and marketing computers and other products that are sleek, colorful, friendly, and fun. Given his legendary marketing prowess, it's a safe bet that his strong *Aesthetic* values are coupled with a no-nonsense practical *Utilitarian* counterpart.

Martha Stewart is another well-known example of someone with a high *Aesthetic* values cluster. A former model, this lifestyle consultant and cooking guru became the epitome of gracious living and creative expression. Her emphasis on creating beauty on a budget suggests that Martha's *Aesthetic* motivation is probably paired with a high *Utilitarian* values cluster. Martha not only surrounded herself with beauty but set a new standard for

---

29

homemakers around the world. Beginning with cooking, gardening and home decorating projects, Martha grew into a popular radio and television personality, with an extensive line of products ranging from wedding planning to musical CDs, signing an agreement with K-Mart stores to feature merchandise from her Martha Stewart Collection.

> *"...One of the attributes of love, like art, is to bring harmony and order out of chaos, to introduce meaning and affect where before there was none, to give rhythmic variations, highs and lows to a landscape that was previously flat."*
>
> *– Molly Haskell*

Without prejudice, it may be fair to speculate that high *Utilitarian* values resulted in alleged insider stock trading, for which Ms. Stewart has been indicted at the time I am writing this book. Think how the harsh environment of a prison might impact someone with a high *Aesthetic* values cluster.

Catherine Carlisi's mother, Kay, exemplifies the *Aesthetic* sensibility in her desire for harmony in relationships, beautiful surroundings, and a thirst for personal growth and creative expression that has kept her enthusiastic and vibrant when others her age have grown bitter and discontented. Kay tends to view events with a true *Aesthetic's* point-of-view. She has dabbled in painting, music, and home decorating, and she awakens each day with a sense of anticipation about what life experiences await her. In fact, Kay is something of a legend in the local golf club, where infighting and gossip were the norm before she threatened to quit her position as club president unless harmony was restored. "Life is too short for pettiness," she told them. "Count your blessings and enjoy each day." Kay also holds the record for eliciting the most hugs in a single day during the fellowship hour at her church.

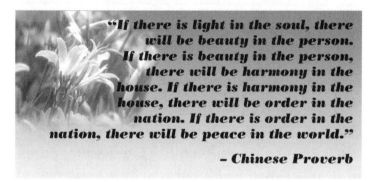

"If there is light in the soul, there will be beauty in the person. If there is beauty in the person, there will be harmony in the house. If there is harmony in the house, there will be order in the nation. If there is order in the nation, there will be peace in the world."

– Chinese Proverb

Dreamers, artists, poets, inventors, philosophers, and other creative individuals are often guided by a strong *Aesthetic* values cluster from their early years, while others may "graduate" to *Aesthetic* motivations later in life, after satisfying other driving passions. For example, many of the industrial magnates of the last century became famous as philanthropists in their later years, contributing much to the beauty and art that we now enjoy in municipal parks, museums and other institutions they funded.

Beauty and harmony are not only "preferences" for those with this values cluster; they seem to actually experience negative physical effects from disharmony or unpleasant surroundings. The organizers of a large conference held a few years ago were inundated by complaints from some attendees who claimed that the discordant colors and pattern of the carpet in the ballroom were making them nauseous.

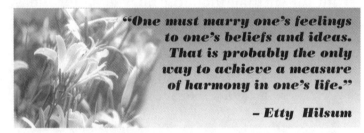

"One must marry one's feelings to one's beliefs and ideas. That is probably the only way to achieve a measure of harmony in one's life."

– Etty Hilsum

However, even those who share a high *Aesthetic* values clusters may not always agree on what is pleasing. For example, some may like Laura Ashley prints, while others may feel smothered by the busyness of the patterns and prefer the simplicity and clean lines of Southwest Native American art.

One of the most dramatic real-life examples on the effects of values cluster conflicts comes from one of my clients. Ann, a female sales representative, came to me to do some self-assessments. She was making more money than ever before yet felt unfulfilled. Ann also had been suffering from an acute case of psoriasis that doctors had been unable to control. After completing the *Personal Interests, Attitudes, and Values* (PIAV) assessment, Ann discovered that she had high *Utilitarian* and high *Aesthetic* values clusters. Ann was selling truckloads of bark to landscapers, but all she could see was the devastation of forests, rather than sales transactions. I suspected that intrapersonal conflict between these two values was causing her psoriasis. Three months later, Ann quit her job and decided to start her own horticultural and landscape consulting business. Within three weeks, her psoriasis totally disappeared without any medical treatment. Almost five years later, Ann's business and health are thriving.

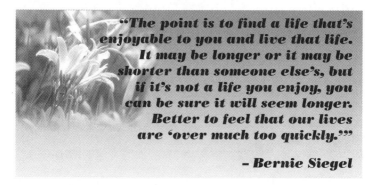

> **"The point is to find a life that's enjoyable to you and live that life. It may be longer or it may be shorter than someone else's, but if it's not a life you enjoy, you can be sure it will seem longer. Better to feel that our lives are 'over much too quickly.'"**
>
> **– Bernie Siegel**

While those with a low *Aesthetic* view may enjoy living and working in beautiful surroundings, they may function well in less than ideal conditions. When assigning workstations, savvy managers consider values-based drives and avoid shutting away high *Aesthetics* in impersonal cubicles without windows.

　　　　　　　　　　　　　33

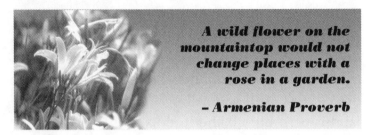

A wild flower on the mountaintop would not change places with a rose in a garden.

– Armenian Proverb

An example of potential consequences for ignoring this consideration involves a man whose company was acquired by another. The takeover leaders lacked sensitivity to the needs of a highly *Aesthetic* support staff and banned personalization of work areas, requiring employees to select one of three standard pictures to hang in their offices. This man, who had formerly loved his job and been quite successful, felt his creativity was being so severely stifled that he quit within three months.

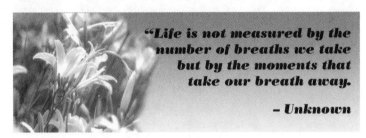

"Life is not measured by the number of breaths we take but by the moments that take our breath away.

– Unknown

On the flip side, at a meeting where a low *Aesthetic* president proudly unveiled the new packaging design for his company's new product line, I was dismayed to see that the new color scheme consisted entirely of gray and blue! When one bold individual commented on the selection, the presiident replied in true low *Aesthetic* fashion: "Gray doesn't show dirt."

Another example of this low *Aesthetic* values attitude is when, several years ago, my office flooded while I was on an extended vacation. When asked what I wanted the staff to do, I sent them a fax, telling them to pick out new flooring, so everything would be installed by the time I returned. One of my employees questioned whether I would like the new floor, and another employee simply said, "Judy wouldn't be able to describe what the old floor looked like anyway." She was correct!

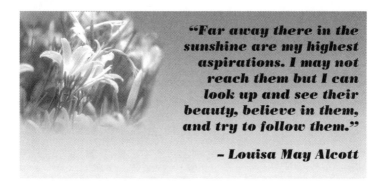

"Far away there in the sunshine are my highest aspirations. I may not reach them but I can look up and see their beauty, believe in them, and try to follow them."

– Louisa May Alcott

Most of the time, the high *Aesthetic* values cluster relates to things like art, dance, music, but can also include things like *feng shui* or aromatherapy. However, it can also be reflected by people who are concerned with the environment—either preserving the natural environment or cleaning it up;

or seen in individuals who demonstrate a commitment to their own personal growth.

SOCIAL
VALUES CLUSTER

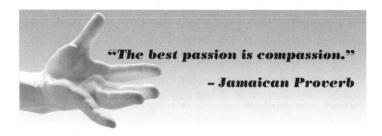

"The best passion is compassion."

– Jamaican Proverb

People motivated by a high *Social* values cluster are often considered the conscience of a community. Many times you'll find them performing volunteer work, such as Habitat for Humanity, or acting as a Big Sister or Big Brother to disadvantaged youth, or advocating for human rights. High *Social* values matched with a strong *Aesthetic* values cluster may find expression in environmental activism.

A characteristic of people with a high *Social* values cluster is that they tend to sacrifice their own needs in order to make things better for others— unless a strong *Utilitarian* or *Individualistic* values cluster modifies that tendency. Those with a high *Social* values cluster go to great lengths in working to eliminate hate and conflict in the world.

Amritanandamayi, known simply as Ammachi, is an Indian woman considered to be a living saint by many around the world. She exemplified the

Social values cluster even as a young child, as demonstrated in this story:

Though her own family was very poor, Ammachi's compassion toward those who were even more in need often prompted her to give away some of her own family's food supplies. Once, when her family had no food, she gave her mother's only gold bangle to a starving man, which resulted in a severe beating when her father found out. Many would consider this behavior to be an overextension of the *Social* values cluster, but despite the beating, Ammachi maintained that she was happy she could relieve someone's suffering. Today, even her parents count themselves among her many devotees.

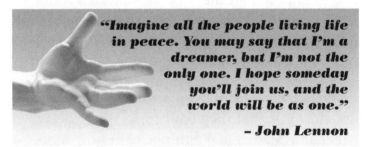

"Imagine all the people living life in peace. You may say that I'm a dreamer, but I'm not the only one. I hope someday you'll join us, and the world will be as one."

– John Lennon

Thomas Moore, distinguished scholar, psychotherapist, theologian, and author, teaches that the cure for many of life's sorrows—loneliness, insecurity, and loss of meaning—are not remedied by finding the right words or getting the right understanding, but in giving ourselves to others. He suggests that we have become a soul-less society because we no longer even give ourselves to our children. Whether you agree with his perspective may be a reflection of how strongly the *Social* values cluster operates in your psyche.

"Charity sees the need, not the cause."

– German Proverb

In her acceptance speech after receiving the Nobel Peace Prize, Mother Theresa exemplified the principles of those with strong Social values clusters as she promised:

"There is so much suffering, so much hatred, so much misery, and we with our prayer, with our sacrifice are beginning at home…And with this prize that I have received as a prize of peace, I am going to try to make a home for many people that have no home."

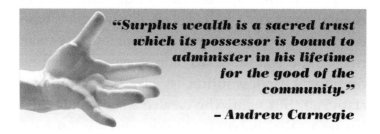

"Surplus wealth is a sacred trust which its possessor is bound to administer in his lifetime for the good of the community."

– Andrew Carnegie

According to Allan Luks, the former head of the Institute for the Advancement of Health, the advantages of a high *Social* values cluster are two-fold. Not only does altruism improve the lives of others, it gives a "helper's high" to the helper in terms of greater mental, physical, and spiritual health.

As President of the United States, Jimmy Carter was deeply committed to social justice and basic human rights. Since leaving office, he and his wife Rosalynn have been promoting peace and human rights through the nonprofit Carter Center in Atlanta. They lead the Jimmy Carter Work Project of Habitat for Humanity for a week every year. "We have become small players in an exciting global effort to alleviate the curse of homelessness," Carter said.

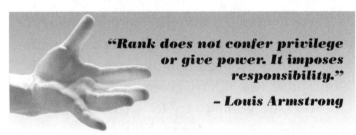

"Rank does not confer privilege or give power. It imposes responsibility."

– Louis Armstrong

As mentioned previously, values clusters can change throughout life, and often individuals who have satisfied their earlier driving needs (e.g., power, money and stability), become impassioned advocates for those less fortunate. Take the example of actor Paul Newman, who created a company to sell his own salad dressing creation and has now expanded to include many other food items, including a line of cookies he called "Fig Newmans." He has donated every penny of his after-tax profits to charity (more than $100 million so far) and during an interview commented, "I have what I need. Why would I need more?" So now, he has turned his considerable talents to what he considers an investment in the community.

> *"Age, health, and stage in life have nothing to do with serving or not serving. In each season of life, there are attributes and qualities of life and experience that God values in service."*
>
> **– Bruce Kemper**

Individuals with a low *Social* values perspective may also donate money or time to non-profit charitable causes, but they may do so out of a sense of guilt or obligation, not because they feel giving to others is part of their life's purpose.

INDIVIDUALISTIC
VALUES CLUSTER

"When you take charge of your life, there is no longer a need to ask permission of other people or society at large. When you ask permission, you give someone veto power over your life."

– Geoffrey F. Abert

With his popular books, such as *Personal Power* and *Personal Power II: The Driving Force*, Anthony Robbins may qualify as the guru of the *Individualistic* values cluster. The high *Individualistic* attitude emphasizes beating out the competition to become number one, rising to the top, winning, and power— and is usually expressed through one of the other values clusters.

For example, someone with predominantly *Individualistic* values coupled with a strong *Theoretical* drive will likely aspire to the highest level of education or knowledge, in order to be viewed by others as an expert. Link the *Individualist* value with *Utilitarian* drivers and you will have someone who strives for great wealth or works to collect the most resources. The expression, "whoever dies with the most toys, wins" was probably coined by a highly-*Individualistic*, highly-*Utilitarian* person. Do you begin

---

to see how our passions influence our life's direction?

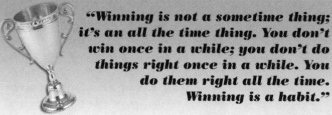

"Winning is not a sometime thing; it's an all the time thing. You don't win once in a while; you don't do things right once in a while. You do them right all the time. Winning is a habit."

– Vince Lombardi

You can probably predict ways in which the high *Individualistic* drive might play out when paired with other values clusters:

When the predominant *Individualistic* values cluster is paired with a high *Social*, the person may become a great philanthropist but, usually, would not be an anonymous donor.

A combination of high *Individualistic* and high *Traditional* may engender a television evangelist or high profile motivational speaker.

A strong *Aesthetic* values coupled with high *Individualistic* might provide the impetus for a world-class art collector or award-winning architect. (A story is told about the time Frank Lloyd Wright appeared in court as an expert witness. When asked to state his name and occupation, he reportedly replied, "I'm Frank Lloyd Wright, and I'm the greatest architect who ever lived. I have to state that because I'm under oath."

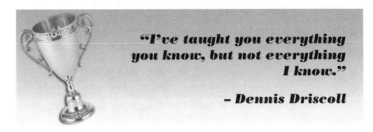

"I've taught you everything you know, but not everything I know."

– Dennis Driscoll

Silicon Valley technologists tell a story that demonstrates the influence that values clusters can have. It is about how Steve Jobs, the entrepreneurial co-founder of Apple Computer, enticed PepsiCo president John Sculley away to become Apple's CEO. With an unerring pitch to Sculley's primary values cluster, Jobs asked, "Do you want to sell *sugar water* for the rest of your life, John, or do you want to change the world?"

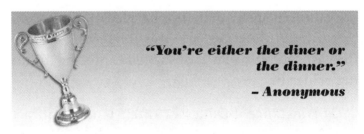

"You're either the diner or the dinner."

– Anonymous

The key to the *Individualistic* values cluster is the strong desire for freedom, especially ability to make decisions independent of what others may think.

People motivated by a high *Individualistic* attitude are generally master networkers who understand the value of power and position and use it effectively.

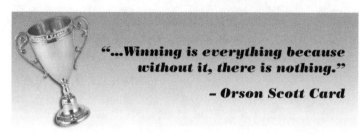

"...Winning is everything because without it, there is nothing."

– Orson Scott Card

In contrast, people with a low *Individualistic* drive often lack desire for power. They may willingly let others take the limelight while they work quietly behind the scenes. "You can accomplish a great deal if you don't care who takes credit for it," is an expression coined by Robert Woodruff, past CEO of Coca-Cola. It clearly describes the philosophy of someone with low *Individualistic* values.

Values clusters can be emphasized or minimized by cultural influences, and it is interesting to note the vast diversity that arises when exploring differing values biases.

For instance, businesses often tend to attract people with homogeneous values clusters. Entire countries often promote the expression of specific value perspectives. The United States has always glorified the rugged *Individualistic*, personified by popular figures such as actor John Wayne and Army

copyright © 2003, Competitive Edge, Inc.

General Douglas A. MacArthur. Around the world, however, these make-it-happen traits are not as well appreciated. I've mentioned Catherine several times, with whom I collaborated on the first edition of this book. She experienced a significantly different worldview when she visited the community-oriented Hindu culture on the island of Bali. It downplays the role of the individual in favor of group contributions.

"Victory has a thousand fathers; defeat is an orphan."

– Chinese Proverb

   This tendency is present in many areas of Balinese life—including the music and entertainment industry, where artists are rarely identified on CDs or in live performances, and no copyright laws exist. Balinese artists find the Western prevalence of single-artist creations peculiar. They ask, "How can one individual excel in every aspect of a great painting?" In the Balinese art world, each artist specializes in a particular talent, creating or mixing paints to create a rainbow of beautiful colors, envisioning and sketching the "bones" of a scene. Then detail artists will elaborate, or others will draw expressive features on faces in the painting. The final product may carry the name of the art collective, but the contributing artists remain anonymous.

In Bali, an emerging nation that lacks the material abundance of the United States, possessing wealth while your neighbors do without is considered shameful. Even in the poorest villages, limited resources are happily shared. Though such a concept seems strange to us, the result in Bali has been one of the most enduring community-based cultures in the world, having survived for thousands of years. Certainly, greater value is placed in their *Traditional* and *Social* attitudes than in their *Utilitarian* and *Individualistic* tendencies. Different cultural values biases create different results, each with their own strengths and limitations.

"You're either getting smarter,
faster, and stronger,
or you're getting dumber,
slower, and weaker."

– Veronica Ross

TRADITIONAL
VALUES CLUSTER

"Who you are is how you live."

– Yiddish Proverb

The *Traditional* values cluster used to be referred to as "religious" or "regulatory," but subsequent research revealed that strongly held systems for living are not always religious, or even spiritual, in nature. The underlying principle for this values cluster is living by a set of rules, whether religious or not, and encouraging others to accept the same standards or attitudes. Staunch defenders of principle-based convictions often operate from strong *Traditionalist* values.

Because people driven by *Traditional* values clusters believe that the systems of living they espouse offer intrinsic benefit to others, researchers have discovered that *Social* and *Traditional* values clusters often occur together as a natural pairing in many people's values profiles.

Those with a *Traditional* values cluster are on an eternal quest for the highest value in life. They are willing to sacrifice everything to be true to their beliefs.

"Better to die standing than live on your knees."

– Yiddish Proverb

Many who have strong *Traditional* values are willing to crusade to support or promote their beliefs. The Reverend Billy Graham is perhaps this country's best-known example of someone with a high *Traditional* values cluster. Since 1947, he has followed the Biblical injunction: "Go ye into all the world and preach the gospel to all creation" *(Mark 16:15)*, and reports cite that he has converted over 225 million souls in almost two hundred countries. Part of Billy Graham's enduring popularity may be that he's not a fire-and-brimstone preacher or pontificator. As an advisor to all recent presidents, Graham is considered not only a great religious leader but one of the most influential men of our time.

Unlike Billy Graham and other moderate public figures with strong *Traditional* values clusters, there are also those, such as some fundamentalist Christian groups and political activists, who are known for aggressive efforts to convert others to their points of view. Taken to extreme, the *Traditionalist* values cluster is prone to intolerance and can even result in long-standing feuds and bloodshed—such as evidenced by the conflict between Catholics and Protestants in Northern Ireland, or between the Palestinians and Israelis in the Mid-East—just two examples from our time. Many wars have been fought over ideologies, so one can see how powerfully our values clusters can influence even the course of history.

> *"The tendency of liberals is to create bodies of men and women of all classes detached from tradition, alienated from religion, and susceptible to mass suggestion mob rule. And a mob will be no less a mob if it is well fed, well clothed, well-housed, and well disciplined."*
>
> **– George Eliot**

But not everyone with strong *Traditional* values clusters attempts openly to convert others to their points of view. Sometimes, underlying values are not overtly expressed but nevertheless affect decisions that are made, as in the following example: a corporate executive with a strong *Traditional* values cluster blocked a major charitable organization from soliciting within his company. Though he admitted that this charity supported many worthy endeavors, he was determined to oppose the group as long as they included Planned Parenthood under their umbrella of beneficiaries. His rejection of the pro-choice point of view was so strong that he uncompromisingly held to his position despite the organization's option of earmarking contributions to specified charities. Those who truly value tradition want to see it applied consistently and may be more concerned with the application than the outcome.

"Never give in, never, never, never; in nothing, great or small—never give in, except to convictions of honor and good sense."

– George Eliot

On the other hand, when two conflicting attitudes are activated, *Traditionalists* must often reevaluate the rules of their system of living, in order to support their higher priority. For example, when the same executive was faced with his brother's homosexuality, he chose family loyalty over reject-

"What makes the difference between a nation that is truly great and one that is merely rich and powerful? It is the simple things that make the difference. Honestly, knowing right from wrong, openness, self respect, and the courage of convictions."

– David L. Boren

ing his brother's alternate lifestyle. He continues to love and support his brother, although he steadfastly refuses to meet his brother's partner or to discuss any aspect of the pair's life together.

Check this out—if you were uncomfortable even reading the word "homosexuality," it is highly probable that you respond from a highly *Traditional* values cluster. (This does not mean that all *Traditionalists* tend to have this reaction but that those who have this reaction tend to have strong *Traditional* influences.)

"A people that values its privileges above its principles soon loses both."

– Dwight D. Eisenhower

Individuals with a low *Traditionalist* values cluster have a different perspective—they value *differently*. You might expect to hear these comments more readily from them:

- "I'm not planning to attend the weekly dinner at Grandma's."
- "I'll go where the job takes me."
- "We won't have children until we are much older if at all!"
- "We usually sleep in on Sunday mornings."

INTERACTION OF CORE VALUES

Until now, you may not have devoted much time to considering your motivational values system. Few of us do, until the factors are explained to us. Then we begin to understand that there are differences in the ways people set their life priorities.

To identify others' values clusters, observe where they spend their time, energy, and money. Listen to what they say about the issues that are most important (and therefore motivating) to them.

Sometimes, our highest values clusters have potential for creating intrapersonal conflict. Think about having high *Individualistic* and high *Social* values. These could be *competing* attitudes if we fail to see how they can serve each other effectively. With understanding, they can become *completing* attitudes, as one values cluster either tempers or energizes the other.

Remember, DISC measures *how* a person does things; values tells *why* they do the things they do. Values can affect a person's behavioral style by either softening some styles or magnifying others.

"How we spend our days is how we spend our lives."
– Anne Dillard

"Spend them wisely."
– Judy Suiter

CONCLUSION

Different values clusters are part of what comprises the richness of the human spirit. They inspire us, they motivate us and they bring meaning into our lives. We bring our values with us everywhere, into our relationships, our communities and the workplace. We tend to gravitate toward the types of work and work environments that appeal to our individual attitudes and values. Therefore, the first step toward creating harmonious and productive workplaces is to recognize the corporate cultures in which we operate and to use the sophisticated assessment tools that are available to support the selection process and consistently hire candidates for "fit" as well as for skills.

Inevitably, however, departments with differing values clusters must interact and then the potential for conflict arises. For example, accounting departments are usually organized around the principle of the conservation aspect of the Utilitarian values cluster, while sales, production or human resources may act from very different perspectives. In today's competitive marketplace, businesses that find ways to help employees negotiate differences are better prepared to dominate the marketplace than competitors whose productivity is compromised by internal strife. And the best way to help individuals and groups work collaboratively is

55

through education and training.

Though we may think it easier to avoid those with world-views contrary to our own, it is neither practical nor wise to do so. Understanding our own motivations and those of others can help us sort through the complexity of human relationships and enable us to find a common ground when conflicting interests collide. Through the process, we may find that our own beliefs and values have been enriched through an expanded world-view. In fact, some schools of thought teach that we learn most about ourselves and create the greatest potential for personal growth when we sincerely engage with those who are different from ourselves.

Certainly, a widespread tolerance arising from deep understanding and acceptance of different values clusters would also go far toward relieving many of the social problems that plague our world today. *Exploring Values: Releasing the Power of Attitudes* is a guidebook for those who are ready to accept the challenge and the adventure of creating more meaningful, authentic and rewarding relationships in every aspect of their lives. As with every great undertaking, you'll meet obstacles along the way, but perseverance and an open mind will reveal new pathways of discovery for you. We hope that our efforts to create a map of the new territory will help you enjoy the journey!

ABOUT THE AUTHOR

"Dynamic, supercharged, a walking encyclopedia, compassionate with an emphasis on passion —a passion for work, for people and for life in general." A friend used these words to describe Judy Suiter, whose company's motto, "Be daring, be first, be different," is also her personal credo.

Judy is founder and president of Competitive Edge, Inc., located in Peachtree City, GA since 1981. She started her company with only $58.38 in cash; today, Competitive Edge is recognized internationally as a top human resources training and consulting company specializing in candidate selection, team building, sales training, executive coaching and professional speaking.

She is a graduate of Middle Tennessee State University with a degree in Industrial and Personnel Psychology. She has over 440 hours of advanced study in behavioral sciences and organizational development.

Judy is also the author of *Energizing People: Unleashing the Power of DISC*, based on William Moulton Marston's research on the four-factor behavioral model. She also wrote *The Ripple Effect—How the Global Model of Endorsement Opens Doors to Success*. With Bill Bonnstetter and Randy Widrick, she is co-author of *The Universal Language—*

DISC Reference Manual, currently in its 9th printing.

Judy has two grown sons, enjoys travel and golf, and is known by many as a gourmet cook. She also believes in giving back to her community. For the past three years she has served as a mentor for the Georgia 100 Mentor Program. Judy is a member of the American Business Women's Association, having twice been selected as the Business Associate of the Year. She was Woman of the Year for 1997, and is past president of ABWA's McIntosh Chapter.

In 2000 and again in 2001, *Women Looking Ahead* news magazine selected Judy as one of the "100 Most Powerful and Influential Women Business Owners in Georgia." She also serves as an advisor in the Chairman's Club for one of her key suppliers, TTI Performance Systems, Ltd. Because she is willing to share both her knowledge and herself with others, Judy Suiter is recognized as a role model and a leader in business.

THE IMPORTANT THINGS IN LIFE

A philosophy professor picked up a very large, empty mayonnaise jar and filled it with rocks about two inches in diameter. He asked his students if the jar was full. They agreed it was.

The professor poured pebbles into the jar, shook it gently, and they rolled into open areas between the rocks. He asked the students again if the jar was full, and everyone agreed it was.

Next, the professor poured sand into the jar, filling every small space. He asked once more if the jar was full, and the students responded with a unanimous "Yes."

Then, he poured water into the jar, filling the empty spaces between every grain of sand. The students laughed.

"Now," the professor said, "I want you to understand that this jar represents your life: the rocks are the important things that if everything else was lost, and only they remained, your life would still be full.

"The pebbles are the other things that matter, like your work, your house, your car.

"The sand is everything else—the small stuff—and if you put sand in the jar first, you won't have room for the rocks or the pebbles.

"The same is true for your life. If you spend your time and energy on the small stuff, you will never have room for the things that are important. Take care of the rocks first—the things that really matter. The rest is just sand."

— *Author Unknown*

Energizing People—Unleashing the Power of DISC is the first volume of Judy Suiter's trilogy on human behavior, which also includes *The Ripple Effect: How the Global Model of Endorsement Opens Doors to Success* and *Exploring Values—Releasing the Power of Attitudes*. This book explains the four behavioral types of people you work with and live with—along with each type's preferred ways of dealing with problems, people, pace, and procedures.

- Because DISC is a *predictable* behavior model, this book explains how you behave and what to expect from others, once you understand their behavioral type
- The value of being able to predict your actions and the reactions of other people under different sets of circumstances allows you to have a greater sense of control over your own life
- This understanding is tremendously beneficial in career counseling, conflict management, job matching, succession planning, team building, and stress reduction

Energizing People is available from Competitive Edge for $9.95 each, plus shipping and handling, or from the Associate from whom you purchased this book. Quantity discounts are available.

The Ripple Effect: How the Global Model of Endorsement Opens Doors to Success teaches you how to build strong networks of support through increased influence and credibility. The principles of endorsement are at work all around us, and Judy shows you how to recognize and cultivate them. This book reveals

- Sources and resources of endorsement—what endorsement provides for people, organizations, and nations
- Five elements that impact the level of endorsement enjoyed by people, organizations, and nations
- Five steps to improving your personal and professional endorsement
- Ways in which endorsement leads to improved performance through the Law of Reciprocity
- What causes loss of endorsement and how to regain it
- Specific methods for measuring and raising your level of endorsement

The Ripple Effect is available from Competitive Edge for $9.95 each, plus shipping and handling, or from the Associate from whom you purchased this book. Quantity discounts are available.

Managing for Success® is the computer-scored, online behavioral style assessment that unlocks the mystery of your natural and adapted styles by measuring the four factors of DISC. The report, over 20 pages in length, can be delivered to you via e-mail in PDF format, is compatible with any computer, and includes

- General and specific characteristics of your style
- Your value to the organization
- Dos and Don'ts for communicating
- Your ideal environment
- Self-perception and how others perceive you
- Keys to motivating and managing you
- Areas for personal and professional improvement

The applications for this information are unlimited and can be used for sales, customer service, team building, conflict resolution, interpersonal skills, management development, stress management, and marriage and family communication improvement.

Managing for Success® and *Personal Interests, Attitudes and Values* assessments are available online from Competitive Edge at a nominal cost, and group discounts are available.

Competitive Edge, Inc.
P.O. Box 2418 • Peachtree City, GA 30269
Office: (770) 487-6460 • Fax: (770) 487-2919
www.competitiveedgeinc.com
E-mail: judy@competitiveedgeinc.com

We accept Visa, MasterCard, and American Express

JUDY'S FAVORITE BOOKS

It's said that leaders are readers, and readers become leaders. I've been asked which books I have found most beneficial to my professional and personal life. I have many helpful books in my library, and I recommend these enthusiastically:

The Platinum Rule: Discover the Four Basic Business Personalities—And How They Can Lead You to Success by Tony Alessandra, Ph.D., and Michael J. O'Conner, Ph.D. Publisher: Warner Books, 1996.

Managing by Values—Becoming a Fortunate 500 Organization by Kenneth Blanchard, Ph.D., and Michael O'Connor, Ph.D. Publisher: Blanchard & O'Connor, 1995.

Developing Leadership & Character—Knowing Enough About Yourself to Lead Others by Drea Zigarmi, Ken Blanchard, Michael O'Connor, and Carl Edeburn. Publisher: Zigarmi Associates, Inc., 2000.

Healthy Pleasures by Robert Ornstein, Ph.D., and David S. Sobel, M.D. Publisher: Addison-Wesley, 1989.

Mind/Body/Health—The Effects of Attitudes, Emotions, and Relationships by Brent Q. Hafen, Keith J. Karren, Kathryn Frandsen, and N. Lee Smith. Publisher: Allyn and Bacon, 1996.

The Immune Power Personality by Henry Dreher. Publisher: Plume Books, 1996.

Between Two Ages, The 21st Century and the Crisis of Meaning by William Van Dusen Wishard. Publisher: Xlibris Corporation, 2001.

Strategy of the Dolphin by Dudley Lynch and Paul L. Kordis. Publisher: William Morrow, 1988.

Unlimited Wealth—The Theory and Practice of Economic Alchemy by Paul Zane Pilzer. Publisher: Crown Publishers, Inc., 1990.

Values Shift—The New Work Ethic and What It Means for Business by John B. Izzo, Ph.D., and Pam Withers. Publisher: Fairwinds Press, 1957.

Self Matters—Creating Your Life from the Inside Out by Phillip C. McGraw, Ph.D. Publisher: Simon & Schuster, 2001.

Play Like A Man, Win Like A Woman by Gail Evans. Publisher: Broadway Books, a division of Random House, Inc., 2001

21 Leaders for the 21st Century, How Innovative Leaders Manage in the Digital Age by Fons Trompenaars and Charles Hampden-Turner. Publisher: McGraw-Hill, 2002.